BOOKS BY GUILLAUME WOLF "PROF. G"

- *You Are a Message*
- *You Are a Circle*
- *reDESIGN: reCREATE*

For information about the author, creative workshops, and additional content, please visit **www.ProfG.co**

YOU ARE A CIRCLE

A VISUAL MEDITATION FOR THE CREATIVE MIND

GUILLAUME WOLF "PROF. G"

SECOND EDITION

Texts and art: Guillaume Wolf.
Copy editor: Kristin M. Jones.

Web content. *You Are a Circle* comes with additional online content. This limited, complimentary offer is open to all purchasers of *You Are a Circle*—to access the Web content, you must have a valid e-mail address. This offer is limited to *You Are a Circle* only, and additional content and registration is subject to availability or change. By providing your e-mail address, you give the author permission to send you information on products, news, and services. In order to protect your privacy, the author does not sell, share, or trade the subscriber list with anyone for any reason. E-mail is never sent unsolicited and is only delivered to users who have provided their e-mail address in agreement to receive these e-mails. You may unsubscribe at any time. Although the offer is complimentary, the participants will be responsible for the electronic equipment needed to access the content. Neither the publisher nor the author shall be liable for any loss of profit or other commercial damages, including but not limited to special, incidental, consequential, or other damages. The terms of this offer can be changed at any time.

A portion of the proceeds from this book will be donated to charity.

For Margaux,

with all my love

THIS IS NOT REALLY A BOOK.

This is an experience, **a visual meditation on creativity and life**—just for *you*, my creative friend. This is a moment of peace, inspiration, and introspection.

You can just look at the circles, and let them speak to you; or you can read the little aphorisms and ponder them. Start from the beginning, the middle, or the end—do *whatever* you want. This is *your* moment.

This is an invitation for you to find the courage to create (because it's not always easy). Push yourself; bring beauty and meaning into your life and the world; share your gift. This is **the way of creativity**, and I invite you to embrace it.

Shine on, little star. Shine on.
Let your light out.

With love,
Guillaume Wolf "Prof. G"

You are a circle
expanding
from one cell
into who you are today.
Remember,
you are a circle
expanding.

Art is what
you make of it.
Life is what
you make of it.

You are courageous.
I compliment you for doing
something creative.

Start where you are now.
Do what you need to do for this moment only.

We all need stories in order to live.
Create a story.
Tell a story.

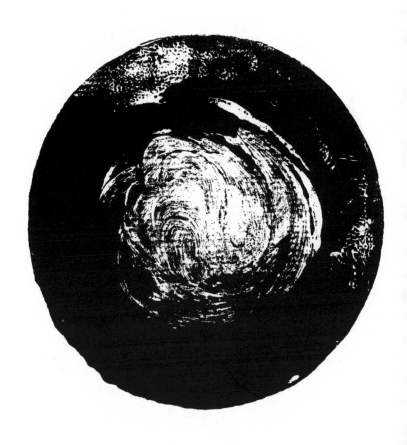

Art is not easy, but it nurtures your soul.

Don't ask permission to create your art. Own it.

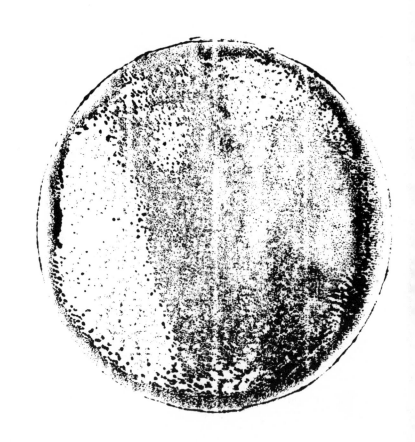

Higher creativity is a leap from the thinking mind
to the transpersonal mind.

It may sound strange, but try this:
Stay out of the way of your own art—
let the ideas flow in as if you were not there.

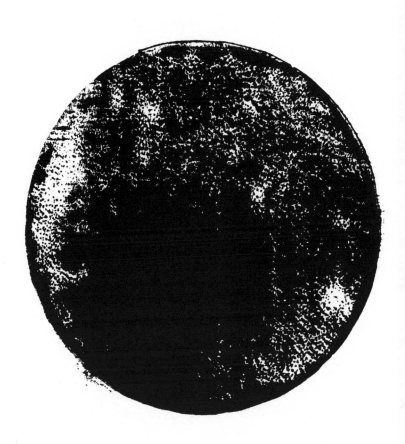

Your inner critic is like a senile relative,
raving mad at a banquet table.
Ignore him entirely and keep creating.

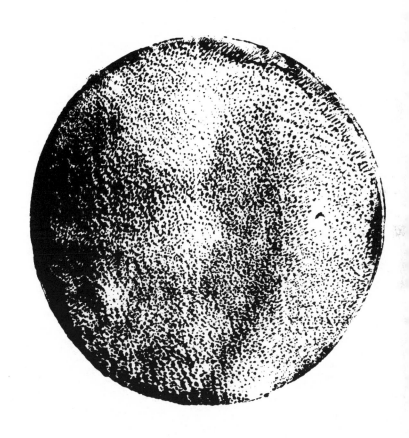

Imagine something big.
Now double it.

Be a fearless artist *today*—not someday.

Create.
Create.
Create.

Today's harshest critics
can easily become
tomorrow's biggest fans.
And vice versa.

Don't worry, it's okay to be weird.

Can *you* do something poetic?
Can *you* do it, in public?
Can *you*?

Your creativity is an ongoing process.
All you have is your process.

Close your eyes.
Take a deep breath.

Feel better?

Think universal.

Look deep inside.
There's a point of stillness
—it's radiant.

Don't be afraid to open up;
people respect that.

Less excuses.
More art.

At Nike, they have a weird motto: "Be a sponge."
It means being inspired by things that have
nothing to do with your domain.
Being immensely curious.

So, you want to be the best?
Be a sponge.

If you fail,
try again.
If you face ridicule,
try again.
If they say "no way,"
try again.
Never stop.
Try again.

You have everything you need to handle your art.
You have everything you need to handle your life.

Can you sing?
Can you draw?
Can you dance?
Can you perform?
Can you tell a story?
Yes, you can.

You are
a circle
living in a square,
creating
triangles.

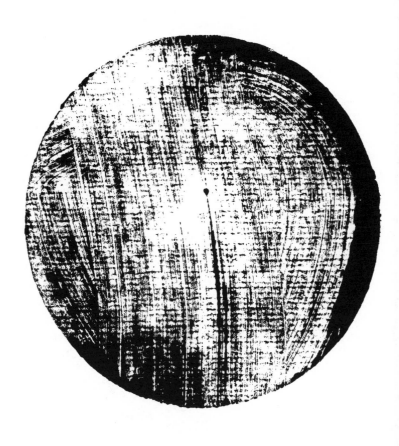

You can heal this.

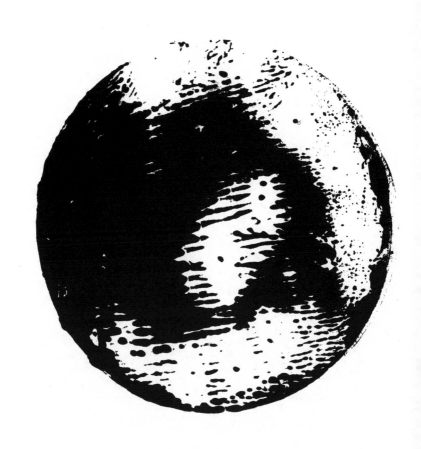

You're scared or unsure about your art?
Get over it.
Do the work.

Know the culture you're in. Be curious—*seriously*.

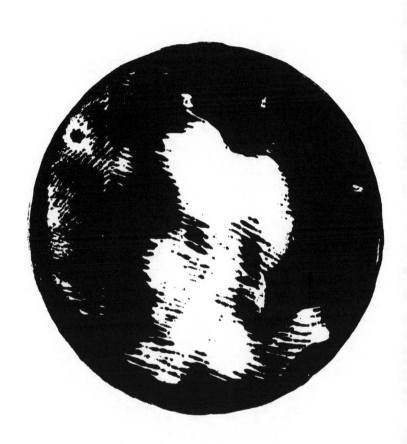

If you get bored,
perfect your technique.
If you get bored,
start a collaboration.

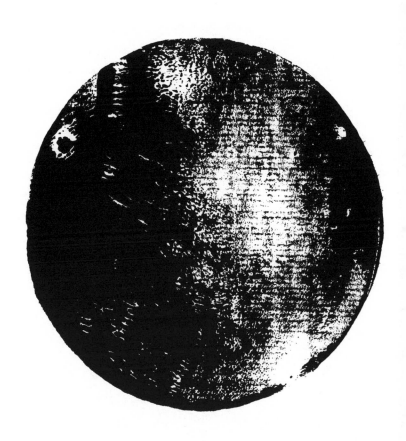

It takes one to know one.

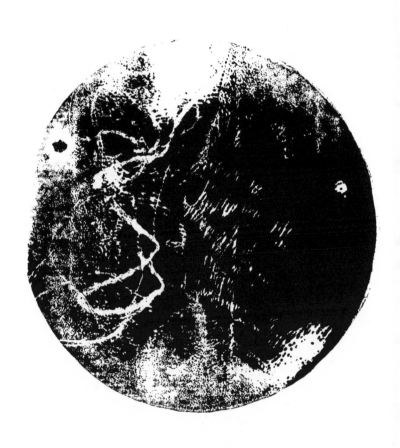

Embrace your insanity—refine it—and bring it into your art.

The future of communication
is both experiential and immersive.

Interestingly, it must also be honest.

I once lost everything.
I remembered that I still had my creativity.
Then I regained everything.

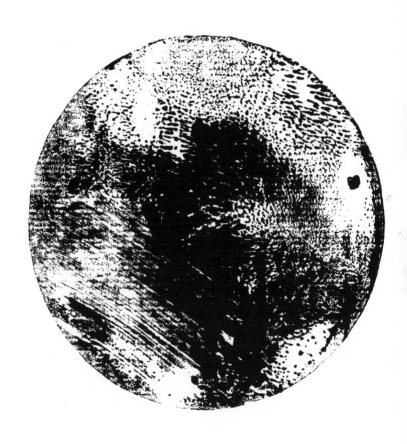

Never forget that your art has to seduce an audience.
Strangely, you're in the business of seduction.

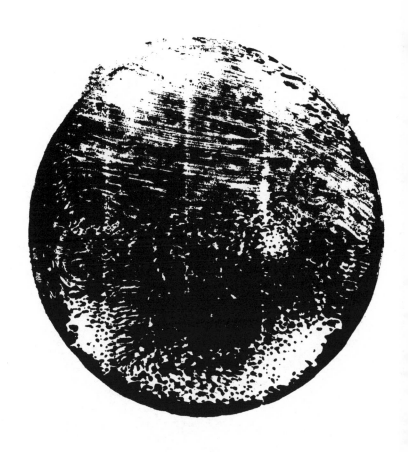

Can you create emotions with your art?
Which ones?
How often?

Do not ever,
ever,
try living
someone else's life,
dream, or passion.
It can't be done!

The air conditioning
plays a strange
melody.
The street provides
the rhythm.
Listen—
everything
is music.

Nurture your body with good food
—it will affect the quality of your thinking.
Everything is connected.

There's always a new way
to look at something.
Try a different
perspective.

Defy time.
Work against a clock.
See what you can do in just one hour of complete focus.
See what you can do over a weekend.
You'll surprise yourself.

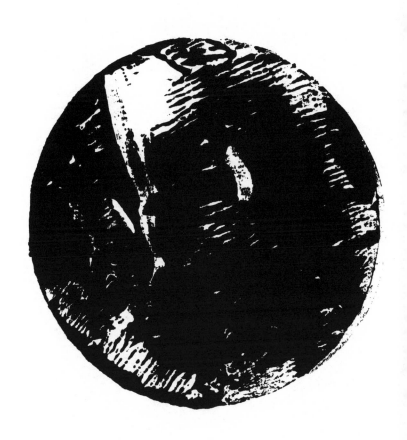

Get lost in time.
Reset a clock to a random time;
follow it and see what happens.

There's a new idea
waiting for you.
Do you see it?
It's coming.

Cut out interesting words from a magazine.
Arrange them randomly in front of you.
Let your mind find a new pattern.

Enthusiasm is creative jet fuel.
It's what keeps you going when times are hard.
Cultivate it.

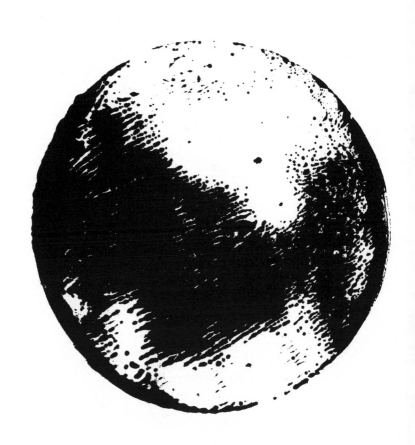

Never take on clients who are doing things
that are against your views.
I was once approached by a tobacco company
that asked if I would help them create a new cigarette brand.
I just said no.

So can you.

When you present a project,
always speak with confidence.
Your energy is contagious.

How can you do that?
Here's the secret: It's just like theater.
Put on a show. And . . .
Rehearse.
Rehearse.
Rehearse.

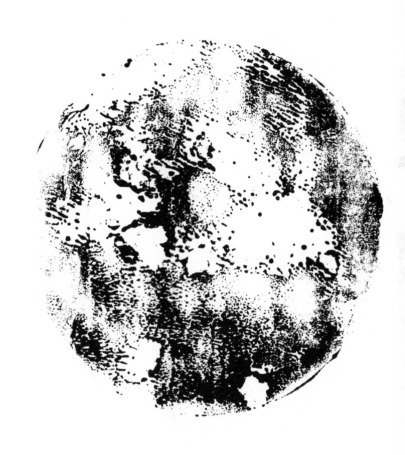

Life is an infinite movement of creation.
When you're creating, you're one with life
—you're truly alive.

If you feel you "don't belong," create your niche.
"Not belonging" could be a great starting point
for your success story.

The secret to creative longevity?
Let your life follow the archetypal journey.

p.s. Study the work
of Joseph Campbell.

If it's made with plastic,
can it be replaced by wood?
If it's made with wood,
can it be replaced by bamboo?
Question everything.

Study big trends.
These are the opposite forces that are shaping our world.
Minimalism vs. maximalism.
Analog vs. digital.
Holistic vs. materialistic.
Organic foods vs. processed foods
. . . the list never ends.

Could you embrace a trend and become its ambassador?

Once you've produced a piece of art,
it's your duty to promote it as if your life depends on it.
Because it does.

Several times in my life
I turned around difficult projects
by using storytelling.
All the best creatives in the world are storytellers.
Study this craft very closely.

Never think you're too old
to start something new.
Never think you're too young
to start something new.
Whatever age—you're good to go.

• here

• here

• here

• here

• here

• here

• here

• here

Remember,
infinity is
everywhere.

• here

• here

• here

• here

• here

• here

• here

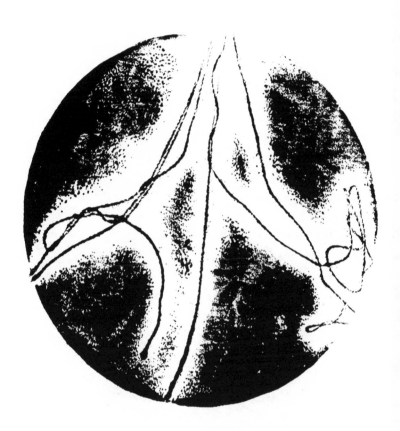

Learn to improvise solutions on the fly.
How?
Use whatever works for now.

Are you stuck creatively?
Look deep, my friend,
until you find your dragon.
Don't let your fears
prevent you from creating.
Do it anyway.
Let's see what comes up.

When I meet students for the first time,
I tell them my class is like a pirate ship:
"We're going to conquer the impossible
and surprise everybody."

The "pirate ship" is the story around which
we arrange our behaviors and expectations
—it creates incredible results.

What are the metaphors you've created
for your life and your art?

Support others in their creative process.
We're all in this together.

You already know that
judging people is a game of fools
because you can never predict what someone
can or *can't* do.

So why do you keep judging yourself?

You are so much more
than what you see.

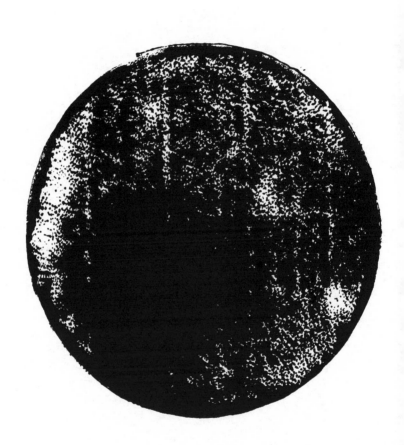

We need more creative people
to find creative solutions.
The world needs you.

Sometimes, creative talent
is being expressed through vehicles
such as caring, or connecting with others
—and that's beautiful.

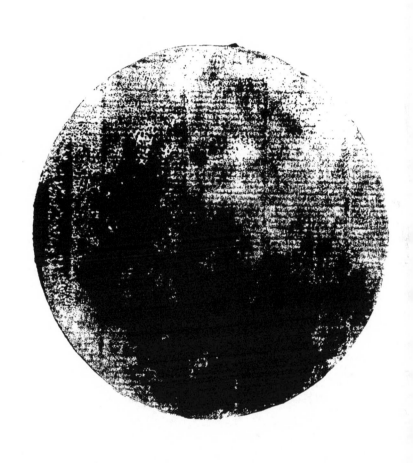

Remember that you are part of our great collective story.
When you decide to empower your reality
with love, creativity, and courage,
it affects us all.

When you open your heart and project your
enthusiasm into life, you create a small opening
for grace. Something in you changes, and life
around you changes as well.

Envision, empower, create.
This is the core of infinite creativity. Practice it
in your life and you'll grow stronger and wiser.

It's not just about what you can do;
it's about what can flow through you.

It's early,
Everyone is still asleep,
You take a deep breath—the air is cool.
4, 3, 2, 1.
You start walking.
Each step sings a melody.

You've found the secret path.
You've found the way.

Look around
—everywhere there's beauty.

Making art is a process of wonderment
driven by boundless expansion.

These are times of creative fluidity when the boundaries
between creative domains are blurred.
It's not really about what medium you choose
or the category you're in anymore, but one thing remains:
You've got to have a strong voice.

Our level of awareness creates how we perceive reality.
If each day you decide to raise your awareness
and bring your focus into everything
that you do or experience,
life empowers you.

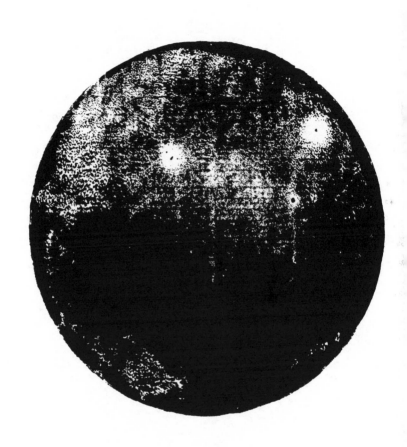

The visibility of your creative career boils down to this:
In what way are you unique and relevant in your field today?
In what unique way are you promoting yourself?

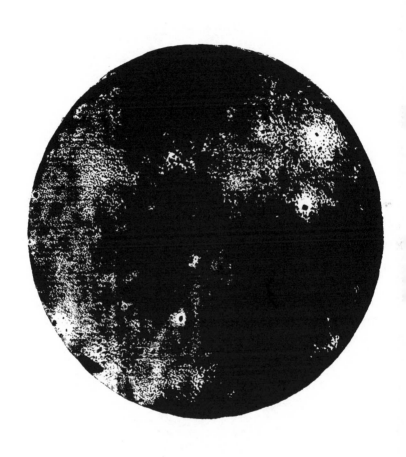

Your energy can light up a room . . . shine on!
Your heart can nurture many . . . love intensely!
Your soul can touch the world . . . let your spirit roar!

Every time you face doubt, fear, or frustration,
find the creative space within yourself
that knows no boundaries.
Listen to what it says.

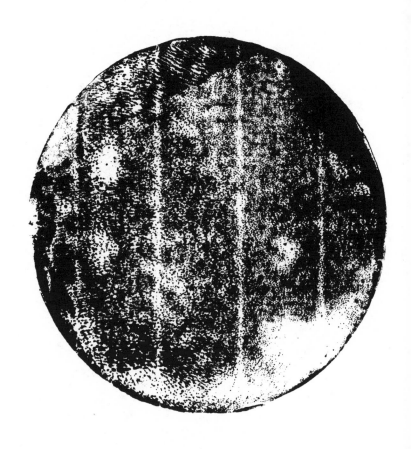

Gratitude is one of the most profound tools for transformation. When you make a habit of counting your blessings, you center yourself within your heart—you enrich the relationship you have with life.

Be grateful that you're walking on the creative path. It is a gift.

Darkest night,
through the fright,
shine your light,
with all your might.

The obstacle you currently face is *not* insurmountable.
If you look at it from a different perspective,
you might see it as a signal to move to the next stage in the
evolution of your life. What are you ready to unfold today?

It's okay to say NO. By saying NO (or no more) to the things, experiences, or people that do not support your well-being and growth, you take a stand for your life.

Your NO can become a creative gesture.

By saying NO, you create a new space of possibilities, and you open new doors for what you truly desire.

It often takes a few NOs to create a big YES!

Learn to say NO.

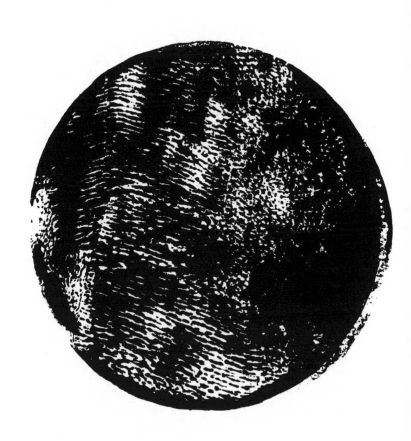

The art of living is simple: it can be taught in three breaths.
First breath: You realize that your life is not in your past.
Second breath: You realize that your life is not in your future.
Third breath: You realize that your life is happening right now.

There you are with the tiny feet.
What can I tell you?—something witty . . . quick!
I wish I knew all the secrets,
but the art is in discovering (for yourself)
this curious game called "life."

(for Margaux)

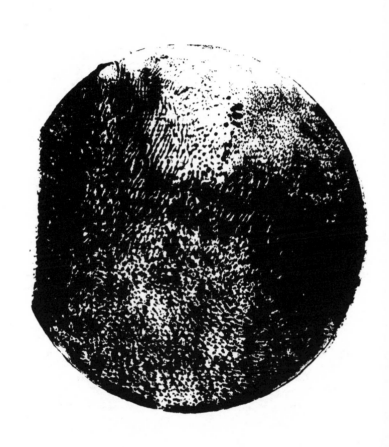

Here's something magical:
The instant I recognize and honor the creative spark in you,
the instant I see it unfolding in front of my eyes.

The experience of freedom comes once you realize that life is not about having the most, but about needing the least —by simply enjoying what is.
In art or in life, it always comes down to finding the essence. The treasure reveals itself when you find the core.

The meaning of life
is whatever meaning
you bring to life

—bring something good.

When you integrate within yourself the idea of movement,
the fear of the future disappears.
Tune in with this movement; become movement itself.

Don't be afraid
of your dark side.

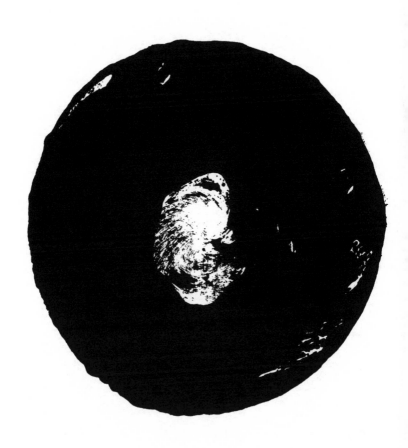

Creative life is a thread that unfolds into infinity.
Every day becomes an invitation for learning
and growing into your best self.

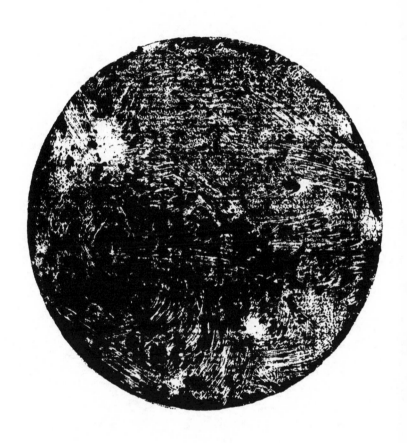

Life is mysterious and full of surprises.
Sometimes life hits us hard.
All we can do is welcome the moment
to the best of our capacities,
do our absolute best with what we have.
And if each day, we're fully present and engaged . . .
if each day, we add a little bit of creativity,
a little bit of love to everything we do
—that's a great way to live.

Pause and look ahead—embrace your horizon.

Move beyond your doubts.
Jump over your fears.
Focus.
Get back to work.
Try again.

We shape our identity with each passing moment.
Can you reinvent yourself?
You're already doing it, *right now*!
All your thoughts sculpt your identity.

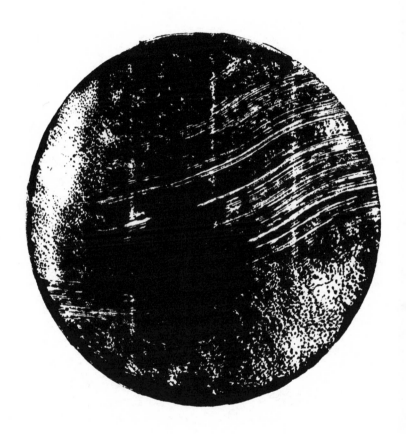

We sometimes forget that words represent qualities
—and that these qualities influence us.
In many ways, words shape our reality. . .
Choose your words wisely.

When you pay attention and reflect
on the infinite combination
of events and coincidences in your life,
you can recognize a pattern emerging.
Follow the thread of this story
—what does it say?

As the hero of this story,
what can you do next to evolve and grow?

Forget yourself in a single moment of full awareness.
That's the magic of art and life.

Less is more. Simplify everything.

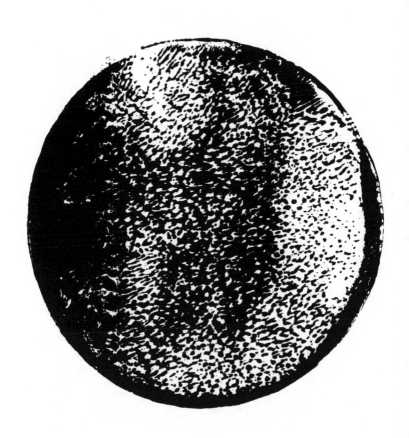

Nature is a temple and we're all symbolic beings.

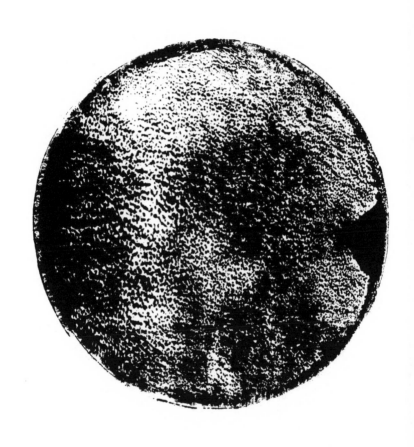

If you can make people laugh,
rejoice—comic genius *is* high art.

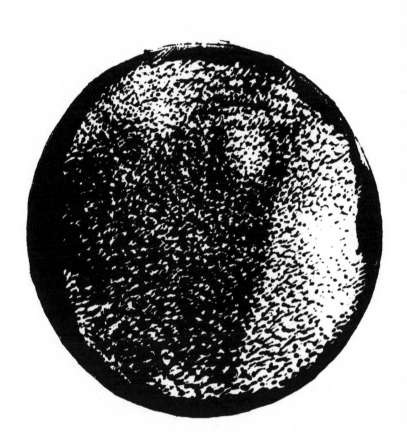

"Finding your voice" is an oxymoron.
Look—it's there already.
You're perfect as you are.

There's a lot of pain in art,
and the way out of it is *through* art.

B.B.E.
Be yourself.
Believe in yourself.
Express yourself.

(Repeat.)

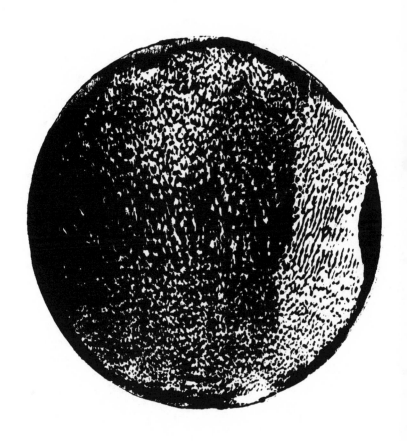

Learn to love people who are different from you.

Be gentle with yourself.
It's important to relax a bit.

Introducing the three projects juggle:

• One project that pays the bills.
• One project that pays for the extras
(that you can land back on if project one vanishes).
• One exciting personal project that pays nothing now
but can have a high impact in the future.

If you learn to juggle these three *simultaneously*,
you'll always take care of the present
and you'll build a compelling future.

Creativity arises from the friction
and synthesis of opposites.

Mix two things that shouldn't go together.
See what happens.

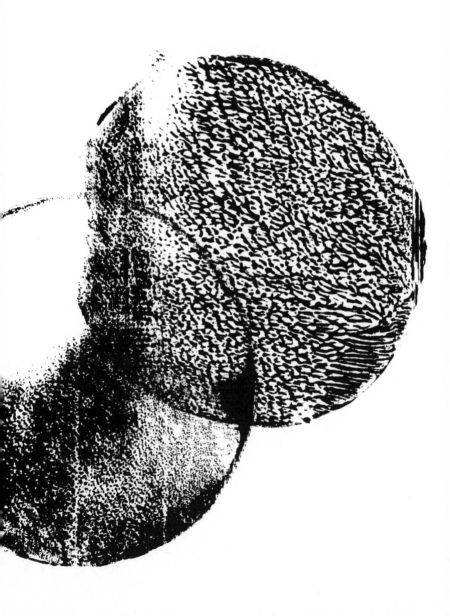

Creative life is like a marathon through uncharted territory.
And if you open your eyes and pay attention,
it's also an inner journey of personal transformation.

Develop
your eyes,
your ears,
your body,
and your mind,
until you can
see,
hear,
feel,
and think
like no one else.

Don't be obsessed with perfection.
It doesn't exist.
Just do the best you can.

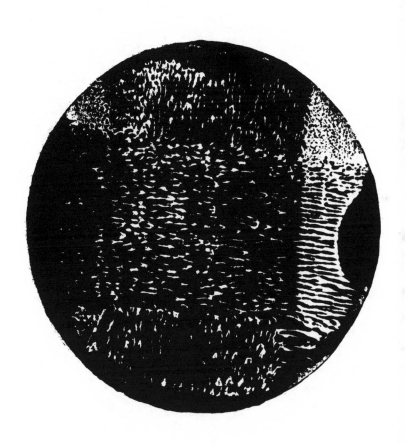

Don't be scared of being copied.
It's actually an honor.

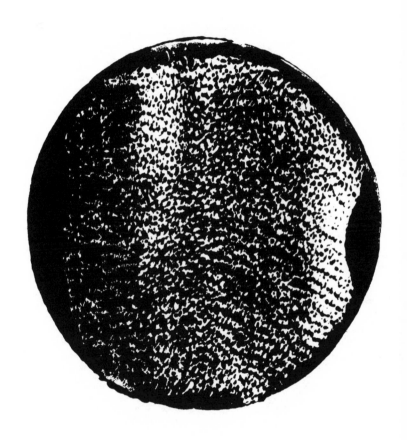

Learn to promote yourself.
You're your best cheerleader.

There's no limit to your imagination.
Think big.
Think how big you can contribute.

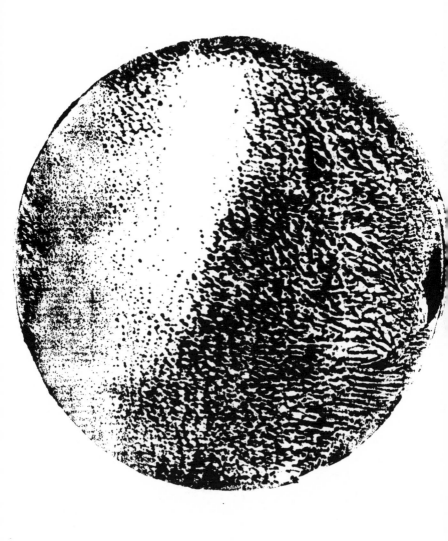

You don't need a beret
to be a good artist,
but being charming
helps your career.

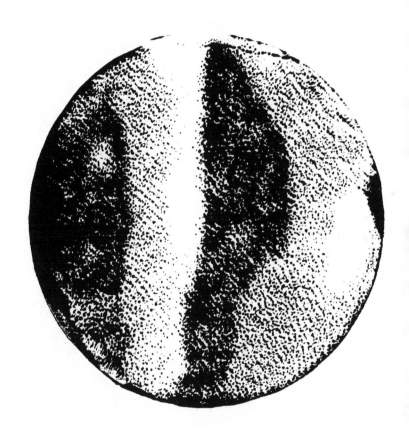

Create something we've never seen before
(I know you can).

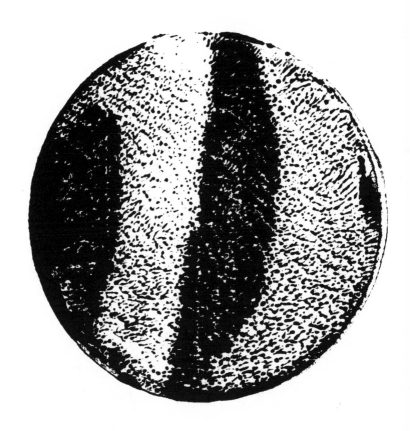

I wonder what you can create in just one hour.

Creativity is a transformative vehicle.
It transforms both yourself and the world.

Play with simple shapes or structures first;
make something out of nothing.

If you can't create because the neighbors
are making too much noise,
get earplugs.

Become what you are—*through* your art.

Go to a café
and observe people.
What's their story?

When you meet someone new, ask yourself,
"What do I like about her?"
Once you've found it,
communicate to *that* part.

As a creative, make sure you're savvy with money.
Save it. Be smart.

Can you create a world I want to become a part of?

"Creating your niche"
means coming up with something
that no on else can do as well as you.
This is the ultimate goal.

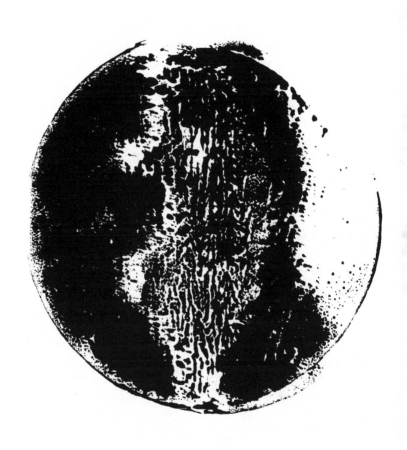

This may sound like a cliché, but remember:
If there are no opportunities around you,
create them.

Ask yourself:
"How can I help them?"
"How can I surprise them?"
"How can I create smiles on their faces?"

Creation is reinvention.

If you think you know everything,
you're dead as an artist.

Your creative career should evolve over time.
Try new things, always.

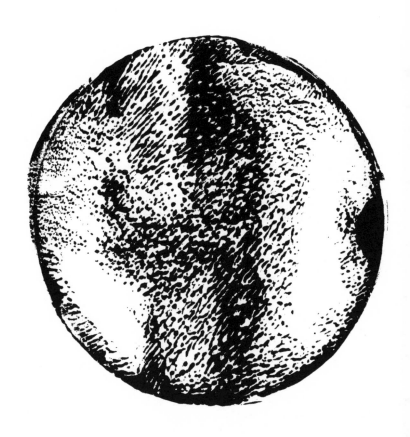

It's okay to think a lot, but you need to act a lot too.

Drugs will *not* make you more creative.
They will either dumb you down or kill you.

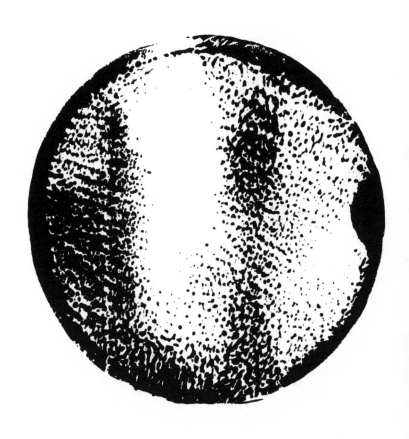

Even if you're small, you can be strong.

MIND   HISTORY

YOU

                EMOTIONS

        HOPE   SUSTAIN

                        SHIFT

            LOVE

                    HOME   PROGRESS

CHANGE

                COMMUNITY   PEOPLE

                    EXPLORE

                            FAMILY

Connect the dots.

                        LEARN

        ART   FUTURE

            FRIENDS

                        VISION   HEART

        PASSION

                    SOUL   NEW

CREATE

            WORK

                                MONEY

            MASTERY

                        NURTURE

        TRENDS

Be candid. Speak your truth.

You can be both completely introverted
and socially graceful.

If someone doesn't like your work, think, "Whatever."
Find someone who will.

Never fully trust an agent.

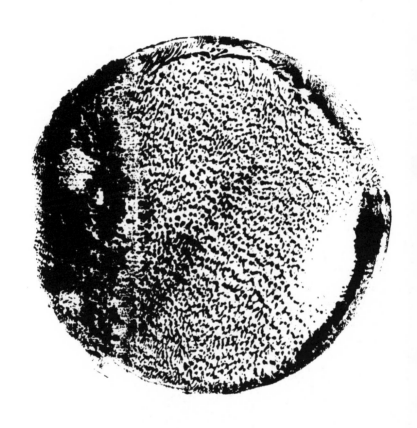

Always read your contracts before signing them.
If you see something weird, ask for it to be changed.
Contracts are just templates for an agreement;
they can be modified if needed.

Watch old movies.*
Read strange books.

Get away from your computer.
Create something with your hands.

Treat yourself. Buy art that you love.
Great creatives collect their peers' work.
When we support each other, we all win.

Music is natural food for the soul. Nourish yourself.

Get into the habit of sketching.
Try 1,000 ideas on paper.
Sketch some more until something great comes up.

Can we all enrich our lives,
create happiness,
and make a difference with creativity?
Absolutely.

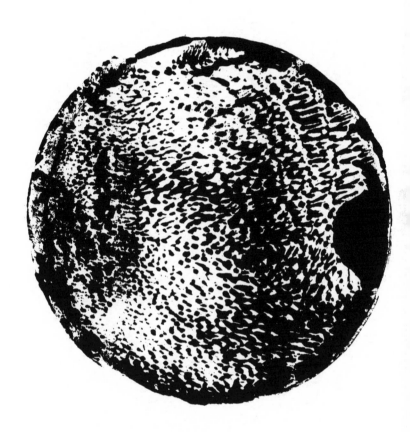

You are a circle
whose circumference
has yet to be measured.

What are you waiting for?

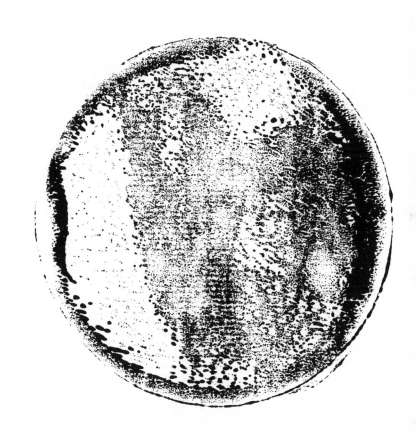

Tabula rasa
(Blank slate)

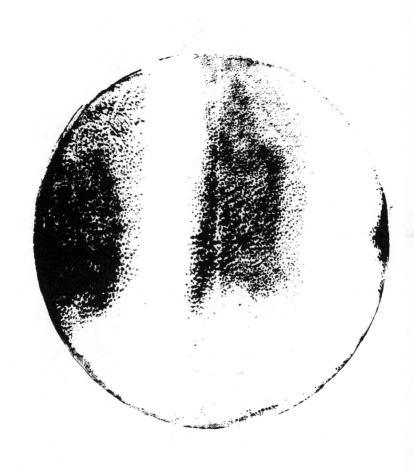

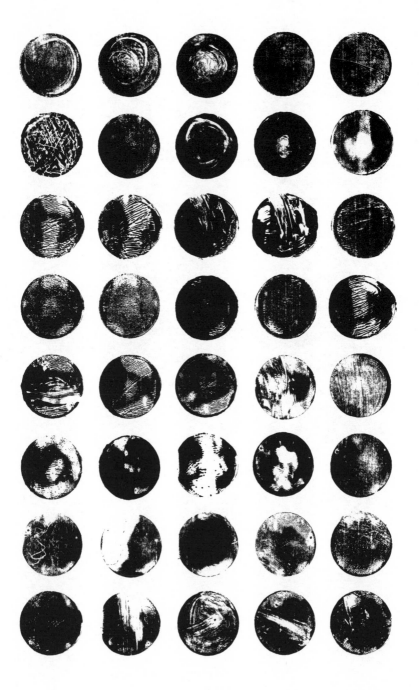

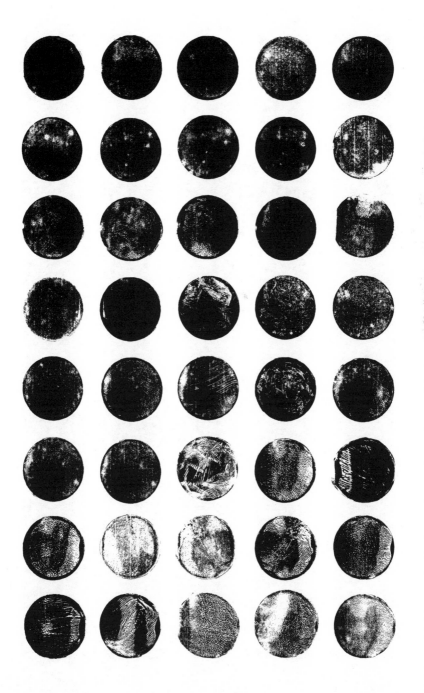

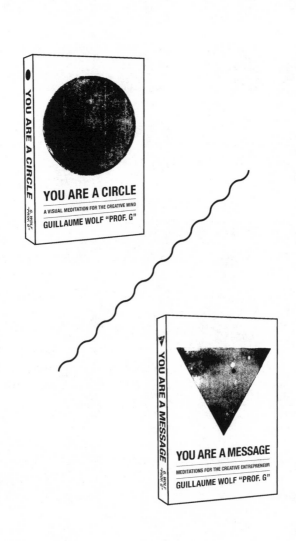

YOU ARE A CIRCLE

● YOU ARE A CIRCLE

YOU ARE A CIRCLE
A VISUAL MEDITATION FOR THE CREATIVE MIND
GUILLAUME WOLF "PROF. G"

G. WOLF
"PROF. G"

▼ YOU ARE A MESSAGE

YOU ARE A MESSAGE
MEDITATIONS FOR THE CREATIVE ENTREPRENEUR
GUILLAUME WOLF "PROF. G"

G. WOLF
"PROF. G"

A MESSAGE FROM GUILLAUME

Hello, creative friend,

I hope you've enjoyed exploring this concept book and that it will inspire you to go out there and do great things.

This book and its companion, *You Are a Message*, are part of the little creative experiments I've talked about in this volume.

<u>What you have in your hands *is* an experiment in publishing:</u> It's inspiration, learning, and art combined. It was done alone: self-published and self-promoted.

Today many professionals still believe self-publishing is impossible. And my goal is to see if, *together*, <u>we can make the impossible become real.</u> These experiments can only work if <u>we partner together as a team</u>. In that sense, this book is symbiotic: It belongs to *you*.

I write *and* illustrate these books on my free time. I'm a teacher and a dad, and I also have a design/consulting practice; but every day, I work extra hard to create projects to inspire other creatives. So if you really like this book and want to see more in the future, please join in and support it.

What you can do: Simply post about this book on your social media platform: Use **#youareacircle** and **#youareamessage**. And, if you're inclined, feel free to leave a review on Amazon.com—it really helps, and it's super-nice to hear from you.

I really appreciate your support.

Thank you
Guillaume "Prof. G"

ABOUT THE AUTHOR

An author, teacher, consultant, and visual artist, Guillaume Wolf is a branding and communication expert.

Wolf trained as a designer and communicator. He is known for his acclaimed creative direction work for fashion and luxury brands. In his private consulting and design practice, he advises brands and organizations on brand ideation, creation, identity, and communication.

A preeminent expert in applied psychographics, Wolf is a full-time faculty member at Art Center College of Design in Pasadena, California, where he teaches communication design and the psychology behind branding.

Wolf is the author of several books on creativity, including the indie hit concept book, *You Are a Circle*, and its companion, *You Are a Message*.

www.ProfG.co

MORE?

Are you curious to discover more?

For workshop information, and complimentary content, please visit: **www.ProfG.co**

Made in the USA
San Bernardino, CA
06 December 2015